"HOPE" IS THE THING WITH FEATHERS

Frank Pugliese

BROADWAY PLAY PUBLISHING INC
New York
www.broadwayplaypublishing.com
info@broadwayplaypublishing.com

"HOPE" IS THE THING WITH FEATHERS
© Copyright 2001 Frank Pugliese

All rights reserved. This work is fully protected under the copyright laws of the United States of America. No part of this publication may be photocopied, reproduced, stored in a retrieval system, or transmitted, in any form or by any means, electronic, mechanical, recording, or otherwise, without the prior permission of the publisher. Additional copies of this play are available from the publisher.

Written permission is required for live performance of any sort. This includes readings, cuttings, scenes, and excerpts. For amateur and stock performances, please contact Broadway Play Publishing Inc. For all other rights please contact the author c/o B P P I.

First published by B P P I in June 2001 in *Plays By Frank Pugliese*

First editon, this book: August 2020
I S B N: 978-0-88145-784-1

Book design: Marie Donovan
Page make-up: Adobe InDesign
Typeface: Palatino

"HOPE" IS THE THING WITH FEATHERS was first produced by The Drama Department, opening on 2 December 1998. The cast and creative contributors were:

BOY	Keith Nobbs
GIRL	Paula Garces
MAN	Avery Glymph
WOMAN	Cynthia Nixon
OLD MAN	Robert Hogan
OLD WOMAN	Maria Tucci

Director .... Randolph Curtis Rand
Set & projection design .... Wendall K Harrington
Costume design .... Jonathan Bixby & Gregory A Gale
Lighting design .... Kirk Bookman
Sound design .... Jerry Yager

CHARACTERS

BOY. *He is half Italian-American and half Puerto Rican, but grew up on the streets. He is anywhere from fifteen to seventeen. He is a little con artist.*

GIRL. *She is Latino. Also fifteen to seventeen. She loves to dance, and is very shy. She has a hard time speaking. She has bounced around from foster home to foster home until she found the* BOY.

MAN. *He is African-American, in his early thirties. A professor as well as an anthropological cook. He searches the world looking for indigenous recipes.*

WOMAN. *She is in her early thirties, a frustrated writer. She is an on-again off-again heroin user. Whenever she gets in trouble she calls the* MAN.

OLD MAN. *He is a doctor, but was a theology student who dropped his studies when he met the* OLD WOMAN. *The* WOMAN *is his daughter. He has stopped eating at this point, upset and self-reflective by the events that happened in his examination room.*

OLD WOMAN. *She is second generation Italian-American. She loves to cook and dance and have sex. She is tough and steady and sometimes so scared she can't tell anyone. She is trying to get her husband and her daughter to speak.*

DEDICATION

To my grandparents

(The scenes of this play overlap, often to the point of being simultaneous.)

(A naked WOMAN *reads from a bed. As she reads, the lights come up on a* BOY *suspended in mid-air.)*

WOMAN: A blue sky. Day. A boy. Fifteen, maybe sixteen. Hair burnt from the sun. Burns that remind you of summer. The last days of summer. Before the first early night chill. A smile he can't wipe off his face. A smile that gets him in trouble. A smile that gets him in love. A smile you turn away from. …At first he is a speck in the blue sky. He floats, as though gravity was not an argument for him. We see he's falling. A pack on his back. He smiles his smile. He reaches for his cord. It looks like a rope from a lamp. It looks like he's going to turn on the light. He decides not to….

(A naked black MAN *enters down right holding a sheet wrapped low around his waist with one hand and a glass of water in the other. He moves center approaching the bed down left.)*

MAN: …Don't look at me that way.

WOMAN: It's like…. You're not listening.

MAN: I'm just. Baby… It's just…. I'm still hard.

WOMAN: So, so what? You can't pay attention with an erection?

MAN: Jesus. It's just, I haven't seen you in a month and you wanna read me this shit, like right after we fuck.

WOMAN: Maybe I get inspired.

MAN: Maybe I am too....

WOMAN: ...And it's not shit!

MAN: I didn't mean. It's just....

WOMAN: This is not for the rag. It's for me.

MAN: I'm sorry....

WOMAN: Whatta you smilin' at?

MAN: You want the water or what?

WOMAN: I want the what...?

MAN: You always want the water....

(MAN *looks at* WOMAN, *looks at the glass of water, and pours the water onto his chest. He puts the glass down on the floor, then joins her in bed, lying on top of her while she pulls the sheet over them. The falling* BOY *speaks.*)

BOY: First it feels like flying. You can't even tell you're falling. Fuck, it's like goin' up, not down. Serious, you think, "Why can't I just stay up here, like, like fuck, forever. Just float. I always like stuff like this, a rollercoaster, I can go on, four, five times in a row. As long as I ain't eaten, like right before... But even then, what the fuck, I don't mind a good heave. I like it. Like after drinkin' all night. Fuck I like throwin' up, it makes me feel "clean and pure." I'm a person who likes experiences, right.... I even climbed into a hippo cage at the zoo. Fucker was so old, couldn't even see me. Like I used to get fucked up not for that lost in space feelin', but for the virginity of it. The pop of the skin. The pin goin' in. The head, that was gravy.... But that's another thing. I'm always thinkin' of other things. It's a problem.... You know, fuck, I could pull this cord and all that pops out is a ribbon comin' out of your back. You come down like that shit that falls out of the sky on the Fourth of July. And this fuckin' instructor tells me what to do. I hate people tellin' you what to do, even if he is a fuckin' instructor. He says later, "You pull the cord more than once you get a ribbon." ...Always liked ribbons, saved every one, off every box I ever got... I ain't got too many ribbons. Fuck him, I'll pull it when I want....

(Lights come up. A pregnant GIRL with dark, curly hair enters down right, crosses center. She sits and wraps a box with ribbon.)

GIRL: "Sun, sun, sun...
Sun, sun, sun...
Sun, sun, sun..."

BOY: I was on the train going down to no place special except warm. And I hear this chick. Chick or bitch. The word, depends on the temperature. 'Cause I got no fuckin' heat in this joint down on Clinton that I share with this junkie "bitch," and her works, and her scabs, and her stupid thoughts. Which she thinks it's okay to speak out, every one every time... Like this one time when she says...

GIRL: "Sun, sun, sun..."

BOY: ...that if you put coffee up her cooch, after she put me up there, she wouldn't get pregnant. Black, two sugars... And she never did...get pregnant. She "got..." me, sick.

GIRL: "Sun, sun, sun..."

BOY: Over and over and over... From the God damn T V commercial kinda song that those four old fags from England sing, the ones with the Mo haircut. You know, "The White Album"... My ass. What a pussy title. If I ever make an album, I'm gonna call it, "The Fuckin' Album!"

GIRL: "Sun, sun, sun..."

BOY: ...WILL YOU LET IT COME ALREADY...?

GIRL: "...Let it come..."

BOY: And she looks at me with eyes the size of C Ds, and she just smiles. An ear to ear number, that got me right between my tits. Like somebody stuck a knife in my heart. Only when they pull it out, I laugh. That knife is the closest thing to love I ever felt.

(Lights come up on an OLD MAN *at a dining table. He takes off his belt, picks up an ice pick to give himself more belt holes.)*

OLD WOMAN: *(O S)* Custard!

OLD MAN: How's your eye?

OLD WOMAN: *(O S)* It feels good on your teeth.

OLD MAN: No.

OLD WOMAN: *(O S)* There's some old bread.... You love old bread, and soup. I made you the soup! And, you can put the bread in the soup. You love that. A soup sandwich.

OLD MAN: Just water.

OLD WOMAN: *(O S)* It ain't really like eating. It's more like drinking....

OLD MAN: No, thank you...

OLD WOMAN: *(O S)* ...What are you doing with that ice pick? You got no ice.

OLD MAN: What?

OLD WOMAN: *(O S)* I can see, you know. I still know how to see.

OLD MAN: I'm putting another hole in my belt.

OLD WOMAN: *(O S)* I DON'T GIVE A SHIT! *(She enters down left, wearing dark glasses to cover a black eye.)* I'm still gonna set the table, before she gets here.... *(She exits down right.)*

OLD MAN: I've had six holes in this belt my whole life. Now I have seven.

(OLD WOMAN *re-enters down right with a tablecloth and begins setting the table.*)

OLD WOMAN: Seven. Eight. Nine. Ten. Till it can fit around your skinny little neck!

OLD MAN: I've only had one car accident. Back then, after the accident, I thought I'd have so many. But I only had one. I've, we've been to Italy four times. Rome three... God, and I thought I would go to Rome whenever I felt it. I been to the hospital five times. I've been to the hospital more than Italy. All these things that I can count on one hand.

OLD WOMAN: Numbers are mean and nasty. They don't care about nothin' or no one. Numbers are selfish bastards! (*She exits down left.*)

OLD MAN: I stopped thinking I was a dolphin by the time I was three. I stopped riding a tricycle at six. Early. My father love bicycles. I stopped believing I had imaginary friends that spoke in a language that blinked like the stars out my window when I was seven.
I stopped being in love with Linda when I was fifteen. When she laughed at me when I put my hand down her pants and ripped them trying to pull it out. I stopped washing dishes in the University cafeteria at nineteen. I said, "Fuck this." I stopped smoking at twenty-one, one year after I started to impress a girl in my Italian class who always wore a scarf.
I stopped wanting to be a priest at twenty-six, three years after I quit the seminary and two years after my daughter was born. Even though I feel like I really made the decision four years before that. I stopped believing I looked like Marcello Mastrianni when I was twenty-eight. Two years after that, at thirty,

ridiculously late, I stopped believing I could play professional baseball.

I stopped helping my daughter with her homework at thirty-one. I stopped competing with my oldest friend at thirty-three, even though he didn't and never did until he passed away.

I stopped playing golf the same year I started, at thirty-seven.

I stopped trying to tell my daughter how I feel at thirty-eight. I stopped pulling the car over on the side of the road to look at a field of sunflowers at thirty-eight and a half. I stopped looking for the coins and stamps I couldn't find in the fifth grade when I was thirty-nine.

I stopped running , at forty-one. Having fights at dinner parties for the sake of the argument at forty-two. Going to movies on a Saturday night at forty-four. Pretending I like cigars when I was forty-five. I stopped believing *The New York Times* at forty-seven.

I stopped thinking about who my daughter sleeps with at forty-eight. I stopped smiling at pretty girls on the street the night before my fiftieth birthday, at forty-nine. I stopped making love with you in the backyard at night at fifty-four. I stopped buying hats and umbrellas the same year because I felt I had enough to last me till I died. I stopped looking through my Atlas that year too... I stopped waiting for my daughter to call me at fifty-three. I stopped swimming in the lake at fifty-eight. I stopped wanting a son, and looking in the mirror, caring about my spots, my wrinkles, or my damn scars at fifty-nine. I stopped swimming in a pool at sixty-one. I stopped walking home from concerts at night in the summer at sixty-two. I stopped going to the office four weeks ago. And I stopped eating three weeks after that.

OLD WOMAN: All this counting. That's all they teach you at school. They teach you how to count. *(Looking at him)* And I swear to you, my old dear sweet beautiful-eyed friend, it's the counting that really tires you out. ...What's next? Do I gotta count the drops from the I V? ...I won't do it. I won't count the clock till you die. I will not sit with you and count! Not with two eyes. And definitely not with one.

(The GIRL pulls out a three-fold greeting card and reads the cover. The BOY is still falling.)

GIRL: "Hope you're feeling much better..."

OLD WOMAN: Count this. *(She flips him the finger and exits down right.)*

BOY: You know why I'm here like this? 'Cause I got a poor attitude. You can't believe how many times I read that shit report card. Piss-poor attitude is what my father said. He wanted me to call him Poppy. Poppy was a pussy.

GIRL: *(Opens the card and reads)* "A cheerful thought like a lovely flower can brighten any day."

BOY: The year we lost the house was the year we all stopped lookin' at each other. And my mother changed all the bulbs at forty. And my father started washin' his hands till they started peelin' off. And I was from California, tellin' them I was from anyplace but where I'm from which is the Bronx, only place with a "the" in front of it. I'm so fucking good looking. I fuck a lot. I fuck all the time. I fuck alotta girls. More girls than guys. Sure, I hate everybody and everything. That's why I'm always smilin', it's the only way to get through the fuckin' day. Everybody likes a smile. Fuck'em.

GIRL: *(She reads the third flap.)* "This greeting's filled with wishes, all sincere as they can be. That soon you'll be well on the way, to a full recovery, and that you'll keep improving, just exactly as you should, until the day when better health is yours again for good!"

BOY: Lemme tell you about me. If I'm walkin' down a street could be a hundred people on that street and some lost motherfucker is gonna come up to me with a backward folded map and ask me, me out of everybody, for directions to some bullshit street with some bumfuck name. And I give him the wrong directions, every time, over and over. *(To audience)* Fuck you, you think 'cause I'm talkin' to you that I like you? You think when I say everybody, it's everybody but you? Fuck you. I hate you too. ...And you too!

(MAN *and* WOMAN *in bed*)

MAN: It's because I'm black.

WOMAN: Don't start that shit again.

MAN: It's because I'm black. Just say it! Be brave for once in this relationship and say it.

WOMAN: I don't want to do this again.

MAN: Say it!

WOMAN: Every time you sleep with me, it's like a broken record.
What snaps in your head when you fuck me?

MAN: You don't wanna be with me because I'm black. I know it. You know it. So why don't you just say it? It's because I'm black.

WOMAN: No, it's because you're a pain in the ass.

MAN: A black pain in the ass?

WOMAN: Do you realize what a pain in the ass thing to say that just was?

MAN: Why didn't you take me to that party?

WOMAN: That book party?! That's like, what? A month ago? ...A book party in L.A. is an oxymoron.

MAN: Don't really want a black man on your arm?

WOMAN: It was business!

MAN: Because a black man is not good business. A party is a....

WOMAN: Work! That's how you write for a magazine. You go to parties and get high....

MAN: I'm starting to feel like a fan, and you're not even fuckin' famous.

WOMAN: Is this? This is about my trip to New York?

MAN: No... Well, yes and no...

WOMAN: My father's house in New York doesn't have much to do with another velvet rope opening on Sunset Boulevard. It's L A. Who the fuck cares if I stick my tongue into your big juicy lips?

MAN: When I was eleven...

WOMAN: ...I do not wanna hear a "when I was" story....

MAN: When I was eleven and I watched Jim Brown make that Kamikaze run in *The Dirty Dozen* in the Chinese Mann, I got a bad feeling about this place.

WOMAN: My father has stopped eating!

MAN: I'm a cook.

WOMAN: My mother is waiting for me, to take him to a hospital... This is not the time to introduce a boyfriend, even if he is my ex-boyfriend, of any color. We're too old to look like some Benetton ad.

MAN: Two months...we lived together.

WOMAN: This time!

MAN: This time was a long time.

WOMAN: This time was supposed to be the last time. …I don't live anywhere.

MAN: Well, your stuff was at my house.

WOMAN: And where were you?

MAN: That's my job.

WOMAN: Well, you travel and I party. That's how we "work".

MAN: I miss you….

WOMAN: I'm not moving back….

MAN: You haven't really moved out yet to move back in. I keep finding your underwear everywhere. I pulled some out of a goddamn coffee pot.

WOMAN: You used to take my underwear off a lot.

MAN: You used to make a lot of coffee. I find stuff all over the apartment. It's like you sprayed. And I can't get it out. …I come home and you're gone, goodbye. Nothing. A postcard of downtown L A. You didn't even write "goodbye"! You didn't even write on a…

WOMAN: What's the point? Half the time you're half way around the world. And half the time, I'm half way…from where I think I should be. Where you goin' next?

MAN: In a couple of days.

WOMAN: Where?

MAN: It's just six months.

WOMAN: "Just!" …Whatever. Even the "over" is over… here.

MAN: Don't be mean.

WOMAN: I'm not mean. I just have a lot of energy.

MAN: …You hear that?

WOMAN: Yes?

MAN: That's children...laughing.

WOMAN: Don't make me sad.

MAN: What is it you hate about me?

WOMAN: A hundred little things.

MAN: Whatta you like?

WOMAN: A hundred little things. And some of them are the same goddamn things.

MAN: Tell me the ones that are both....

WOMAN: You never shut up.

MAN: I hate hotels. You know what people do in hotels? They wait.

WOMAN: Look, I have to deal. ...My parents... It's delicate.... I'm not that intimate with my father....

MAN: ...With anybody.

WOMAN: Fuck you.

MAN: I never see you as passionate as when you tell me to fuck off.

WOMAN: If that's what you want, you got it, a very passionate fuck you....

MAN: Why don't you wanna get married? Why?

(Pause as MAN *and* WOMAN *look at each other.)*

MAN: What do you need? A formal invitation to the question? Maybe if the question was some glamorous party you would come in a designer dress and gimme an answer?

WOMAN: You don't....

MAN: Is it because I'm a...?

WOMAN: Don't.

MAN: ...Is it because I'm a cook?

WOMAN: You're an anthropologist.

MAN: Is it because I'm an anthropologist?

WOMAN: …It's because you're an asshole….

MAN: A black asshole?

(The GIRL pulls out some press clips and reads from one.)

GIRL: A thirty-year-old man decided to kill himself by leaping out of a fourth-story window. Because the buildings windows don't open, the man took a running leap, smashed through the glass, fell forty feet, the branches of a tree broke his fall. He landed on the top of a car that absorbed most of the impact.

BOY: She collects shit like that. You get her scissors and a stack of magazines and she is happy as a good shit.

GIRL: A little dazed but undaunted, the would-be suicide jumped up, ran into the building, took the stairs to the fourth floor, leaped out the window again…and landed through the same tree and onto the same car.

BOY: Monday, that's when everybody tosses them. I tried selling them on the street for awhile, but that's a bullshit gig. The weather fucks with the merchandise. And these J Crew motherfuckers walk up with six bags from The Gap and try to whittle a dollar magazine down to a nickel….

GIRL: He broke both his ankles and could no longer run back up the stairs….

BOY: And for what? Who reads this shit? A six-month-old magazine with some over the hill movie star idiot with a hard-on talkin' about his trip to Cuba, or some other eleven o'clock news bullshit he don't know from his wife's pussy. Cause you know movie stars don't go down… They pay people to do shit like that.

I took her to that big church in the city. For the Irish people. The one with all the Japanese tourists. It was a date, that's right. And I gotta say, I have ripped off that donation box once or twice in my day. My hard-up days. I dig lighting candles. For free. That I dig. *(To the* GIRL*)* Baby, I like light. Christmas in the Bronx. They light up their houses like Christmas trees.

GIRL: I want my house lit up like that all the time.

BOY: Me too.

GIRL: Promise?

BOY: *(To audience)* I ain't never promised nothin' to nobody in my whole fuckin' life. And I say fuckin' for a reason. 'Cause some people have a life. And some, have a fuckin' life.

GIRL: Hey! Promise?!

BOY: I promise. *(To audience)* And I look the place over. Like I was lookin' at it and not her. 'Cause even in this church, I can't keep my eyes off her and how good it made me feel. *(To her)* How do you like this church? *(To audience)* Nothin'. I'm gettin' no play whatsoever. She just shakes her head. She looks the place over. Standin' there, holdin' her little notebook. She carries the fuckin' thing everywhere and every place. It's one of those black marble jobs. The one's where you color in the white spots all year, so by the time summer comes around, you got like an all black book. *(To her)* I said, do you like this church? *(To audience)* And she shrugs. And that's what you get for puttin' yourself out, a fuckin' shrug. I was ready to call it a day, a night, and a whole 'nother day. I was ready to call it a weekend. And I mean "…end!"

GIRL: I like the small tree in the back…

BOY: *(To audience)* …Yard… You could see it from the little window in Saint Patty's john. Yeah, I went in the ladies room. This is New York City, and even if we got any ladies left, I tell you this, they don't mind. …I like to watch her pee. It made me smile. Even a little bird has got to tinkle. And she was sittin' there writin' on the bathroom wall. Hey little bird, what you write on the bathroom wall?

GIRL: "Fire
Fire don't burn wood
Wood
Wood burns fire."

(The GIRL opens her notebook and reads a list from it slowly. She ultimately finishes her list at the same time the BOY finishes his next monologue.)

GIRL: "Long leaf pine, slash pine, table mountain pine, white, black, red spruce, Fraser fir, Hemlock, Cedar, Umbrella, Magnolia, Laurel oak, Myrtle oak, Sweetbay, Rosebay, Redbay, Dahoon, Flowering Dogwood, Cottonwood, Basswood, Paw Paw, Parer, Yard, River birch, Mulberry, Sweet birch, Sugarberry, Nannyberry, Donny serviceberry, American plum, Pin cherry, Chestnut, Carolina silver bell, Slippery elm, Witch-hazel, Balsa poplar, American holly..."

(BOY overlaps while GIRL reads her list of trees:)

BOY: I saw this movie on T V, but this was real. What the... What's that called, a doc...? Black and white shit. And every once and a while some old fucker in a bad suit starts doin' blah blah blah. ...Documentary! Right, motherfuckers. Whatta you lookin' at?! I fuckin' watch public television. It's educational!
The girl in the documentary, she was like raised alone, in a room someplace. They passed her food under the door and shit. She didn't see nothin', or say nothin', she was livin' nothin'. She was locked in. While her old mother was at the A & P buyin' some maxi-pads. And the check-out chick was like, "Fuck, she's all dried up. What's with the pads?" The delivery guy followed her home, and they found this girl. Fourteen years too late, right? Know your neighborhood, right?

This was like that movie with the chick who was the prostitute in that other movie, when the guy who was a boxer in that other movie, shaves his head like the old band the Sex Pistols and kills everybody... like, everybody. Beautiful... He's the fucker on the magazine. What the fuck's his name?
Anyways, like this documentary ain't like the movie. This is like, real. Like really real. Not like in that movie where that prostitute is talkin' like a retard and pointin' up at, who the fuck knows what she's pointin' at?

(GIRL *continues her list of trees in the silence.*)

BOY: Jodie, yeah, Jodie... What the fuck do I care about Jodie what-the-fuck?
In the real thing. This girl lives, it's like a dungeon. Then they gave her foster parents...who can make you crazy as is, let me tell you... But what she does is, like, she collects things. Like somebody's gonna take it all away. Like that! (*Snaps his fingers*) She takes all the glasses in the house, fills them with water, and puts them in her room. When they go in her room. She's got glasses of water everywhere and every place. My girl's like that, she collects happy endings like they was glasses of water. Shit, what is her name..?

(GIRL *rejoins, vocally finishing reading her list.*)

BOY: ...Jodie, Jodie, Jodie, Jodie, Jodie, Jodie... She was in that other movie about the genius kid with the big head, like the guy in Rudolph... (*Serious*) How come I know all this shit about movie stars and shit? How come I know more about them than my own fuckin' here and now?!
You watch T V. Who needs these details?
Entertainment bullshit and Lifestyles of the Crap.
Get it out.

GIRL: "Sweetgum, Sugar maple, Sycamore, Sassafrass, Shiny Sumac, White ash, Winterberry…"

BOY: *(To audience)* …She really likes trees. *(To the* GIRL*)* Why do you like trees so much?

GIRL: They grow, even in the winter….

BOY: …I went to school.
I tried.
I even dated my English teacher.
My problem was spelling. And it ain't my fault. 'Cause spelling has got no mother. Words don't spell the way the goddamn words sound like…or should. According to me!

GIRL: How you spell it?

BOY: I-M-U-N-I-T-Y.

GIRL: Like electricity.

BOY: They were the first ones to shut us off. Then the phone. The gas… Do you see what I'm sayin'? How come nobody teaches me how to pay the bills? How to do a checkbook. First and last month's rent. How much a doctor cost when you got no insurance. No. I know about Columbus and 1492, shit like that. Hey, Columbus don't pay the doctor.

GIRL: Jodie Foster… She's famous…'cause she went to college.

BOY: …My girl would hide out in a closet, in a "foster" home where they didn't even remember her name. They didn't even know she was missin'. Now, if you people, the sixty grand a year university ra-ra types, "we know the black man," reach across the tracks shit. You wanna take a kid in? Here's a little tip: you gotta remember the fuckin' girl's name.

(The GIRL *turns to a page in her composition book and reads.)*

GIRL: My boyfriend.

BOY: When she was sixteen, social services finally found her grandma. But by then that lady was so old she kept callin' my girl "the nurse."

GIRL: My grandmother had a white bird. Her very last boyfriend left it with her when he went back to his wife.

(MAN *and* WOMAN *finish dressing.*)

MAN: Is there somebody else in New York?

WOMAN: My father is in New York.

MAN: Maybe somebody like your father, maybe...?

GIRL: In his photo my grandfather has his arms up in the air. His hair is standing straight up. And she told me the secret. He was standing on his hands. That's fake. This bird would fly out of its cage. Fly around. Then sit right on her head. The bird would grab her hair and fly straight up. I swear, she would lift off the ground a little. Just lift. When she dies, the white bird pulled all its feathers out. My boyfriend said the bird walked across the wood floor and fell asleep between her feet, but I know he put the bird there. That's my boyfriend. *(She bows and sits in the center chair.)*

WOMAN: Do you want me because you want me or do you want me so you don't have to want me...?

MAN: What's that supposed to mean?

WOMAN: You're driving me crazy.

MAN: I saw your messages. There's alotta calls from New York.

WOMAN: From my father!!! I been talkin' to him.

MAN: ...About us.

WOMAN: ...About me! ...He's been tellin' me with a story.... This story is the only real talkin' I ever did with my father in my life.... And what the hell do you mean, my messages?

(The flying BOY *speaks.)*

BOY: Things I like.

MAN: It's a man's name....

WOMAN: That's my father's name!

MAN: ...All these years and I don't even know your father's name....

WOMAN: If my father met you, he would die.

BOY: Things I like.

OLD MAN: I know what you're trying to do. I know what you're getting at. Think I don't know? 'Cause I know. And I know you know. I know you know. ... Just. Dear... I hear it. I hear it all too well, all too well.

OLD WOMAN: YEAH, I SEE IT! I SEE IT ALL TOO WELL, ALL TOO WELL!

BOY: Things I like. I like to throw eggs into fans while they're goin'. I like the triangle on a lady when her vagina meets her legs. Shit, I love a vagina. All of it. The way it smells and tastes and feels and looks. I'm a vagina man. I'm the hoochie coochie man... I like car accidents. Not just after, but during. I like to see them, and be in 'em. ...I been in seven. They go so slow. Cool slow. Shit, I can't remember a drive to the corner, but I remember an accident like it was happenin' right now. ...I like takin' lint out of a dryer. Out of the filter... That way it peels off... I like peelin' wax off my finger too...a lot. I like the way ballerinas stand. Their feet out like that. ...But that's about all I like about them. 'Cause they're all a pain in the ass....
I like when bald guys put their hair up and over, rich man poor man. I like that shit, makes me laugh.
...I like scars; I like them a lot. I like to get into one

movie and then watch all six at the joint. I like doin' that with a girl. I like to look at people with my smile, and then stop smilin' and they get all freaked out... But I loved to watch her move, not that I like dancing 'cause I don't. No, I don't. But I loved to watch her locks bounce when she danced around my room in a G-string and her funky wool cap.

(The pregnant GIRL *starts to dance.)*

BOY: I called the winter, the Florida keys. She would be like, "I like..."

GIRL: ...dolphins. When they jump out of the water like that. When you touch them, their skin feels like a nectarine. And their nose. They can find things in your stomach, like a baby. They point at it, under water.

BOY: I had these supers all over the city drop me a key here and there for a nickel and a dime...bag. And she would cook these cookies. And be like, "I like..."

GIRL: ...the roll of dough. The little guy, you push his fat gut in and he giggles. And the whole house smells sweet. That's what bein' rich is like. It smells like chocolate chip cookies all the time.

BOY: And she would lay on the couch eating cookies and look up at me and just talk. On the T V, "I Dream of Jeannie." And she would say like, "I like..."

GIRL: ...Jeannie, because of her style. The clothes. And that little apartment of hers, in the bottle. Jeannie was a foreigner.

BOY: And we would wear just our underwear in these houses. And she would crank the heat up high as can be.

GIRL: I like the heat. It's like Florida. *(Stops dancing)*

BOY: And when my girl would get this room as hot and cozy as a closet, it was the only time on all them couches, in all those apartments, that she got quiet. Don't stop likin' things. Don't! Whatta ya like? What? And she stopped talkin'. I knew what she liked. She liked this dress on the T V.

WOMAN: What?

MAN: Nothin'... It's just we get to this place where I don't know...

WOMAN: What?

MAN: What to say. We always come, get to this place, when, we, I don't know. It's like we talk like we just met. Like other people are listening. Like...

WOMAN: A restaurant conversation... People should eat at home.

BOY: I do these things and it's like. It's like, it's not me. It's like I'm watching myself do them. But I say "myself" like I know who it is. No. It's like I go, "Look at that guy fallin'. He's fuckin' sick." Then after, I'm like, "That was me. That. How can I do so many sick things?" I think that's how people kill each other, with that kinda thinking. That's how I jumped outta this plane. Sky dive my ass. That junkie's check I gave them is gonna bounce better than I am. After a while you ain't floating anymore, you're falling. And it's funny what comes when you fall. I keep thinking about this time when I was like, maybe eight. And I got caught in this navy blue sweater, I couldn't get it over my head. I thought it was tryin' to kill me. I got so scared I pissed my pants. And when I finally got the sweater back down and I walked into this lawn party my parents were having nobody knew what was goin' on with me. My sweater was still on, I was sweaty and red, with a big piss stain in front of me. I guess I think about that 'cause the other thing is hard to figure. Like why I did it with her without protection. Why she let me do it. We were sayin' "love that" all night, lovin' this and that and everything. And why I didn't stop that night was 'cause at first, when I got it in her, it was like, same, it wasn't me. But when I got out it WAS, and she was her, and I was me....

(The OLD MAN *and the* OLD WOMAN *are at the table. She has sunglasses on.)*

OLD WOMAN: *(She takes off her dark glasses.)* You like it?

OLD MAN: Somehow it seems right. It suits you.

OLD WOMAN: Maybe there's something wrong with you.

OLD MAN: Maybe wrong is right.

OLD WOMAN: Loss of appetite can be a symptom of something else. An ulcer or intestinal problems...

OLD MAN: I am a doctor, you know.

OLD WOMAN: That young girl with the hair, she couldn't keep anything down. It kept comin' up. Maybe you caught somethin' from her.

OLD MAN: She's with-child....

OLD WOMAN: I always loved the way that sounds. "With-child." It makes you see, how it's a little love thing....

OLD MAN: She's very sick.

OLD WOMAN: That's very scary. I can see how you would lose your appetite.

OLD MAN: I didn't lose my appetite.

OLD WOMAN: Then eat.

OLD MAN: I chose....

OLD WOMAN: I don't understand....

OLD MAN: And you won't understand!

OLD WOMAN: Forty years I've understood everything. I may not have gone to seminary like you did. I may not read the books I pick up around the walls we call a house. But I understand.... I understand every one of your ticks. I know what you're goin' to whistle from the way your lips come together. I can read your face. So don't tell me I don't understand. Because you don't know what I understand. You don't even know what I know. What the hell happened with that girl?!

OLD MAN: It's like there's water in my ears. It's like splashing, crashing...waves in there.

OLD WOMAN: Those are tears in your ears!

OLD MAN: That's the price you pay for listening.

OLD WOMAN: You know, what you hear when you put a sea shell to your ear? It's not the sea that you hear coming from the shell. It's the echo of your own blood pulsing.

OLD MAN: Where did you read that?

OLD WOMAN: In your waiting room.

OLD MAN: In a magazine?

OLD WOMAN: You sayin' I'm stupid?

OLD MAN: No!

OLD WOMAN: Because I wish I were stupid. I wish! I'd get more sleep.

OLD MAN: The noise is really getting to me....

OLD WOMAN: I was on the bus. And it was when I heard "Sheridan Square". I knew that voice from before. "Breathe in, breathe out." It was our old doctor. Our doctor was driving the bus. And at the front of the bus, at the white line, I leaned in. And saw his glasses. He never saw too good. And I was, "Doctor, why...?" And he turned and spoke when he finally saw me. "Because from my office I couldn't. You see, there is a bird in the jungle no bigger than my thumb. And when it flaps its wings it sounds like a thousand violins." For a long time we watched the trees. He was a good driver. Eyes and all. "Next stop"…our stop. And as I turned up and said, "Better, much better." And the doors shut, and as the bus headed down, I swear, I could hear a tiny bird in my ear.

OLD MAN: Is that story true?

OLD WOMAN: No… But it's good.

(The BOY *lights a cigarette.)*

BOY: What? You think fallin' at like thousands of miles per second I don't got time for a smoke? I do. I tell you what I don't got time for. I waited across the street from that doctor's office for sixteen and a half cigarettes.

GIRL: In the hallway the doorman in a marching band suit was talking to my tits. At the window I filled out a form. Where it said insurance I put my boyfriend's name. In the waiting room I looked in a magazine. Superman is in a wheelchair. On the wall was a butterfly in a glass box. A pin in its back. In the chair across from me a really old Spanish lady had little palm trees on her shirt. On the rug a little boy was puttin' blocks one on top of the other. From the office I smelled smoke. Sweet, smelled like a donut on fire. *(She stares right at the audience.)* I pulled the shade up, looked out the window. My "insurance" was smoking. My boyfriend winked at me.
The nurse made me drop the shade.
She scratched her mustache.
A man with a tube in his throat came out.
In a little white room I could see the purple under my eyes in the steel napkin holder.
I washed my hands with green soap.

On the table was this off-white paper. I wish I had a roll of it. It looked good to draw on.
I took my socks off. My feet looked very little.
I sat on the stool. And it made my ass cold. I kept spinning it around to keep warm.
There was a picture of them three funny brothers from those black and white movies.
They were smokin' a bong.
I heard the blocks fall outside.
The doctor's eyebrows were pointing straight up.
He smelled like burnt toast.
His fingers looked like Italian sausages.
I was holding the socks in each hand so tight it hurt.
He put his sausages through my hair….
I watched one sock hit the floor.

BOY: Let me tell you about the first time a guy touched my dick.

GIRL: When I came running out crying, I was usin' the other sock to wipe my eyes.

BOY: The guy was a computer geek. Never shut the fuck up about "the future is now" and shit. To me they just look like big calculators. I think he'd rather fuck a computer if he could. He was working on a program to break down a painting, then put it back together again, like someplace else. Like, why? He just reached over and put his hand on my dick. Like it was a vegetable he was buying in a supermarket. Like he never felt one before. Not even his own.
He had a bad haircut. When you're on the street, it's always the ones with a shitty trim that come at you. Or they're wearin' sunglasses at night. Or they got a scarf on when it's like eighty outside. They're the ones comin' for you. No way these guys get laid on their own. I hadda pay Doctor Finger's labs in case. Up front. In your face. On the table. Cash is how I get in

the door. So I called Mr Wizard over at the land of the misfit boys where he works. I made believe I was an intern or some student type-shit. He met me on forty-second street. In the doorway of the new Disney Store, where you can buy Mickey's ears, Donald's beak, and my dick.

GIRL: "Come little children see the place Where infant dust must lie There is no age that's free from this Both young and old must die."

BOY: That's her favorite tombstone. She's wacked like that. Makes me laugh.

(MAN *reading from index cards*)

MAN: "It is called the great wall of China. But I believe the greatness lies in the people and animals who live beside it....
There is a mushroom that grows on the edge of this wall. In this damp shade of a thousand years something grows. On the other side of the wall you find in the cracks and inlets of the wall a small nest. Facing the sun to keep its eggs warm."

OLD WOMAN: Oh, and you should go down to the village to the old place.

MAN: Any questions?

WOMAN: No!

OLD WOMAN: His son is there now, but I knew enough about his father for him to hold on to one of those big round loafs for us. The one that reminds you of you know what....

MAN: "...It is the people who live by the wall who find taste from it...."

OLD WOMAN: She doesn't like American bread....

(GIRL *shifts her chair downstage.*)

MAN: "…Nourishment and life. They climb the wall. First to gather the moon-shaped mushrooms and then, after the birds have flown away, to gather their sun-drenched nests. Because you can build what you want, but the will to reach over to survive and touch the other side will never go away…. Any questions?

WOMAN: Yeah… Why do you keep asking that, "any questions?"

MAN: The questions are what's really important. What's a matter now?

WOMAN: You're a better writer than me.

MAN: I'm not a writer. I'm….

WOMAN: …I know. You're a cook.

MAN: I'm a teacher.

OLD WOMAN: Then I think, pasta with broccoli, broccoli rabe.

WOMAN: This whole thing is not a lecture.

MAN: Yes it is.

OLD WOMAN: It reminds me of weeds.

WOMAN: It's like you're trying to seduce someone.

MAN: Damn. You should give this lecture on walls.

OLD WOMAN: Lontano cheese.

MAN: Because you know how to build them.

WOMAN: …Finish.

OLD WOMAN: You can get the cheese in that great place next to the bread man. She likes spicy….

MAN: "The nest is the size of a fist." And they say your heart is the size of a fist.

OLD WOMAN: And then, blood oranges.

MAN: And yet it beats. It grows even though it can, yes, it can shrink.

OLD WOMAN: With sugar. And I don't care if she's the only one who loves that.

MAN: What have we done so badly that we, no, with all our gifts, all our philosophies, our engineering, that we build great walls of China in our tiny hearts...?

OLD WOMAN: And the espresso? Well, espresso. We all love espresso....

MAN: This year I went to China and you will be happy to know that Chinese food is still eaten in China.

(Pause as they look at each other.)

OLD WOMAN: Sometimes I think the only reason you took me with you to Italy is for the recipes.

OLD MAN: I don't wanna go to the market.

OLD WOMAN: I want another Sunday dinner with my daughter because that's what I settled for. I'm not ready to stop eating with you. And my appetite has got to be taken into consideration here!

MAN: ...I know where you can get an apple from China.

WOMAN: Is that a question?

MAN: A Chinese apple. At the farmer's...

WOMAN: I don't wanna go to the market. I have to go home. And I don't even know if I can do that.

(The BOY *and the* GIRL *appear.)*

BOY: We were at City Island. It was after we got the test scores back. Well, I guess they ain't scores. Results. And those fuckin' doctors with their bullshit "I'm sorry's" before they take their alarms and sedans out to Westchester and east chester and every other fuckin' chester. We were havin' fried clams out on that big pier over there. And I could see her lookin' straight up to the sky. I thought she was prayin' or somethin'. So I go, "What?" And she goes…

GIRL: The birds up here are so smart they fly down. But then they stop. They just stop and let us eat.

BOY: But I hadda go, "Baby, there's fishin' line up there. It's clear, spread out on a six-inch clip. Those birds don't fly down 'cause their wings would get all caught up in the line…" And she goes,

GIRL: …Oh…

BOY: And it broke my heart. The way she said it like that. Her eyes, red like that. What, baby, you wanna feed the birds? We can throw it on the rocks. They eat off the rocks.

GIRL: No…

BOY: Somethin' got wrong. *(To her)* You okay? You know, besides the obvious. Besides those asshole doctors, those play-with-your-heart assholes… Then she asked…

GIRL: You believe in miracles?

BOY: I didn't answer.

GIRL: Just 'cause somethin' never happened doesn't mean it won't.

BOY: You gotta know somethin'. I loved this girl more than anything in the world. I would get a smile so big on the inside I looked like I was crying on the outside. And I wanted to. I wanted to tell her what she wanted to hear. But I love this girl. I ain't never lied to this girl, and I never will…. *(To her)* No, I don't. And she looked so sad to me. So sad.

GIRL: Then, but what do you believe in? That's all…?

BOY: That, like, is so hard. And I ain't gonna trick myself with waitin' for a miracle or two. But I didn't say that. That woulda killed us both, right there. I said, whatta you mean, miracle? And she goes…

GIRL: There are all kinds a miracles. Maybe I'm your miracle. Flying is a miracle. Maybe I could make you feel like that. Maybe we could make each other fly no matter how sick we get….

BOY: I looked at her a good long time. And I think that in this life, everybody's got this one question you wish you answered different. You wish you could go back and answer it right. Maybe if I could've cried right there. But no one ever showed me how. That woulda helped. No, I wanted to say yes, but I said no.

(*The* MAN *and* WOMAN *in bed*)

WOMAN: Do you wanna fuck again before you go?

MAN: …What?

WOMAN: How can somebody so smart say 'what' so much?

MAN: Go?

WOMAN: I gotta pack.

MAN: You've never ever even unpacked.

WOMAN: If you're not gonna fuck me, could you at least do me a favor and lay on top of me?

MAN: You talk and it's like I'm sitting here, but I can feel my shoes going on as we speak.

WOMAN: I get so light I could hit the ceiling. Like a kid's party balloon.
I should tie fishing weights to my hands and feet. … Look at all those blankets. I don't know what I need more, you inside me or on top of me.

MAN: Or in China… Do you need me?

WOMAN: I need the weight.

MAN: I could drop the dresser on you.

WOMAN: At least I won't bounce off the walls.

MAN: We could pad them.

WOMAN: Do you know that, sometimes with fucking, hard fucking...the man can hit the woman in the same spot as the Heimlich maneuver? ...If I was choking like on a chicken bone, you literally could fuck me back to life.

MAN: You got any chicken?

WOMAN: You don't like to talk about fucking.

MAN: I hate that word!

WOMAN: You hate the word "fuck" and I hate the word "what". How we ever going to talk about anything?

MAN: You're gonna tell me about your father or 'what'?

WOMAN: My father is the kinda doctor that other doctors send their kids to. I would make believe something was wrong with me just to get into his office.... But, I was never sick enough for 'em. Now even now. ...I been in this room for... I can't pack. I can't get out. My mother's been cooking for weeks. And for what? I can't keep anything down anyways, except a drink. She calls now. She doesn't even talk. She just cries into the phone. My mother is crying and my father is dying....

MAN: ...Whatta you lookin' at?

WOMAN: I don't know. The ceiling...? I'm sorry. This hotel is made out of paper. ...The footsteps. The crying. The bodies... Do you know what it sounds like when a body bounces?

MAN: No.

WOMAN: I didn't either...I've been in here for weeks with my thoughts and things and... I didn't call you because I know...when I leave you get so mad at me. I know. I could see it in your eyes. Even now. If you were that type of person who could hit me, you would. And I been twisting in these sheets day and night. But this place is so loud. Well, you know. Anyways, I have these ear plugs. You listen to ear plugs, it's really swishy. Sometimes you can hear your heartbeat. It can't get out of you. I think it goes through your ears. Sometimes it's your own heartbeat that keeps you up. And I finally fell off last night into a really simple dream. People always have these complicated dreams; an adventure, a cat with a dog's head, whatever. Me? They're always like, "Hi Dad, how are you?"

OLD MAN: Fine, how are you?

WOMAN: And that's the whole dream. And I'm havin' one of those. When I hear a knock. It sounds like someone is knocking on the door with a big mitten. I thought it was winter. It was New York. And I get up and it's not, and I'm annoyed, and I'm missing you, yes, missing you, yes. And I was, like, this fuckin' hotel is so loud. It is going to kill me if I don't get out of here. And I went, and I opened up my drapes to open the window, get some air in. It was so hot. ...I hate air conditioning... They say it makes you sick. It think it makes you stupid. And I see her. On the balcony. Eighteen maybe, maybe seventeen, waiting for her birthday, maybe not. On my balcony, her legs are bent in the wrong angle, going against nature. Blood out of her mouth, nose, ear, even her... And her eyes are blinking.

MAN: Oh no.

WOMAN: But I sat on my bed, my whole body shivering. It must have been close to a hundred and I was freezing. I wrapped the blanket around me. I did miss you, and many other things...but yes. I sat there for a long time. ...I didn't go out to help her. I could even go out that glass door. I wanted to disappear. But I couldn't even get up to get lost. When the cleaning lady came... She looked at me, and I looked at her... And looked at me with this disgust. The police came... Sometimes I wish I could be like them. They checked to see if she was dead. She was, and then she wasn't her anymore. They talked about cheesecakes and barbecues. They literally would bump into her head like she was stone. The chalk outline. The measuring tape, a big white bag. They left her shoes... They left them. Strange.

MAN: That's why you called me back?

WOMAN: The cleaning lady looked at me. She lifted the shoes. Party shoes. A pair of red pumps. And she lifted the shoes. Almost like, "Are they yours or do you want them, or can I have them?" And I said yes. ...Then she washed the blood off the balcony. I watched her wash around the chalk lines. Not wanting to disturb the outline. As if the girl was still there. This woman who barely speaks our language, had more respect for a body than any paramedics, any detective, even the manager of the hotel. I cried then. I wished the cleaning lady would lay me in a tub and wash around my outline, keep me white and clear...couldn't even wipe the tears off. It was so hard to dial your number. My fingers were shaking so badly. But I called....

MAN: ...How did she...?

WOMAN: ...And you always pick up....

MAN: ...I mean...where's my coat?

OLD MAN: Let me see your eye.

WOMAN: The cleaning lady couldn't read this little sheet of paper she found in one of the shoes. It was from one of those small memo pads, ripped out, one end like confetti. All I said was, "wish you were here".

(The OLD WOMAN *with the* OLD MAN*)*

OLD MAN: Lemme see your eye.

OLD WOMAN: Ow! I loved when she was young. And every night when we all ate together... Ow! That was what I loved about the day. Planning the night... Ow!

OLD MAN: How do you get into a fight at your age?

OLD WOMAN: You should see the other guy....

OLD MAN: Hold still...

OLD WOMAN: ...You know that's impossible. No matter how old I get.

OLD MAN: *(Grabbing her face)* Then I'll do it for you....

OLD WOMAN: Anything wrong in there doctor?

OLD MAN: *(Examining)* "The eyes are the window...."

OLD WOMAN: Like my windows, don't you? Wanna jump in for a swim?

OLD MAN: *(Holds up two fingers)* How many fingers do you see?

OLD WOMAN: I see a yellow photo of a young man, wrinkled white shirt, wrinkled pants, even his socks are wrinkled. Wrinkled all over, except his face.

OLD MAN: Well, time took care of that.

OLD WOMAN: It's a Sunday. And he's sitting on a chair instead of a pew. An old chair he found in the trash by the train station in Rome. And the chair sits by the lake, not the ocean. He likes to swim... And the young man is peeling a pear. He eats the peel and she eats the pear. And he says to her...

OLD MAN: "I love a pear...they know how to sit."

OLD WOMAN: Peel me a pear?

OLD MAN: I said, how many fingers do you see?!

OLD WOMAN: I can see! I can see right through you. It's not clear yet. Not cellophane yet. It's not that kind of dying yet. It's like that oil-stained newspaper. The paper we used to wrap the cheese sandwiches in.... That hard cheese. But the bread over there. You loved those picnics.

OLD MAN: No, what I loved was swimming naked at the lake.... Not even that... Not so much the swim I miss, or the naked. But the still you could hear under the water.

OLD WOMAN: And whatya hear now?

OLD MAN: Now it's like when I came out. That moment when you tilt your head to let the water out. But it didn't. It's like that all the time. Tilted...with water.

OLD WOMAN: You know I saved that paper. Il Salvatore. To remind me how poor we were. How hungry. How hungry... We were so poor we couldn't afford a picnic basket. We hadda use your robe. And you know what I always say, robes should always become picnic blankets.

OLD MAN: You were never lonely back then.

OLD WOMAN: We had so many ideas. We ate'em like slices. God we could talk. Like words were water...

OLD MAN: Drops of...

OLD WOMAN: And that is how you make a lake. ... One drop at a time. Do you remember how good those cheese sandwiches tasted?

OLD MAN: Are you trying to remind me how to eat?

OLD WOMAN: I'm tryin' to remind you that you're hungry.

OLD MAN: ...I have to tell you something. That night, after the day by the lake, when we walked looking for a place to sleep. And we climbed over that bombed-out wall....

OLD WOMAN: You, me, the robe. I can still feel the grass on my feet. If someone would ever ask me what wet smells like. It's that grass....

OLD MAN: Who the hell asked what wet smells like?

OLD WOMAN: It didn't smell too good when we woke up.

OLD MAN: That's what I wanted to tell you about. Remember the grass got dry, almost stiff, in the morning. I knew. I knew that was a riding school on that other side. I knew that's where the horses went to eat breakfast. The dry grass.

OLD WOMAN: The wild horses?

OLD MAN: Wild? No, they were the horses from the riding school.

OLD WOMAN: But I tell everyone they were wild.

OLD MAN: Well, that's you...isn't it?

OLD WOMAN: That's how I tell that story, like it's a funny one....

OLD MAN: Let me finish...I wanted to sleep there... Well, we didn't sleep. And I wasn't hungry for food that night, day.... I was hungry for you. My heart, my body, everything. I wanted you under the sky and I didn't care about a rubber raincoat back then when people thought sex was rain. I was so hungry. I wanted to eat you. I wanted to eat you all day. I wanted to make love to you with the horses around us. I wanted to live like that.

OLD WOMAN: We made our daughter that night. "Where the horses come for breakfast." You know...?

OLD MAN: I don't want to talk about our daughter. That's what I wanted to tell you. I knew the horses would be there.

OLD WOMAN: That's all?

OLD MAN: No... When we woke up with all those eyes and nostrils staring at us. I saw. The chair, broken. I swear, I remember it like it was yesterday. One of the horses must have....

OLD WOMAN: That goddamn chair.

OLD MAN: And I know that if I didn't walk out carefully, I would literally break everything. And you followed me.

OLD WOMAN: You blame me for following you!

OLD MAN: Did we live this life like that...? The way we walked out of that field...? I didn't want Sunday dinner to take the place of....

OLD WOMAN: Do you blame our daughter for getting made that night?

OLD MAN: I don't know what to say to her!

OLD WOMAN: Talk to her...

OLD MAN: I tried!

OLD WOMAN: Not at her!

OLD MAN: Goddamn it, I don't know what I'm doing! I don't know what I'm doing here!

OLD WOMAN: But you're doing it to me! ...You're goin' to die!

OLD MAN: Maybe I won't. Maybe I'll just get thinner and thinner until I just disappear.

OLD WOMAN: That's what happens when you die!

OLD MAN: You disappear?

OLD WOMAN: Will you miss me when you're dead?

OLD MAN: What kinda question is that?!

OLD WOMAN: Will you miss me?

OLD MAN: That is so academic.

OLD WOMAN: You know I don't need to get married!

OLD MAN: I know.

OLD WOMAN: I didn't need it. I went to City College for two years. I had friends. So. I want you to know, I didn't need...

OLD MAN: When we first met. When I was going up to your room. In the third-floor walk-up down on Bleecker Street. When we were full of sweat and bad saxophone music. And your eyes were bigger than two moons. And I watched your ass swim its way up the stairs. And I only just met you. But I reached up and put my hand on it. Because I felt blind with possibilities. And I knew without your ass to get me through, I might get dizzy and fall....

OLD WOMAN: It's more of a pillow now than a direction... But this ass is your house. Choose it! Finally...

OLD MAN: Let me put a patch on your eye.

OLD WOMAN: I gotta ask you for something now. ...Put your hand on my ass!

(OLD MAN *puts his hand on* OLD WOMAN's *ass. Then he rests his head on it.*)

OLD WOMAN: Did you get dizzy and ready to fall when you touched that girl?

OLD MAN: Enough...

BOY: We were on the A train. Or somethin' "up" like that. Comin' down from city. The car was back to back. Our back, a pair of after-college frat guy types, paper

shopping bags, brand-new baseball hats, and those new leather jackets that look old on purpose.
My girl is whistlin'.
I like that. When she whistles it reminds me of when you open the window late at night in the summer. But today is tough, right? She sounds more like late spring into early fall, on her way to a radiator hiss. When these frat boys go… *(Doing the voices of two frat guys)*
"Fags and freaks."
"Fuck them."
"If God don't want fags and freaks to die, then why are they? That's all I'm saying."
"Fuck them."
And my girl ain't whistlin' no more….
"What about Magic? He doesn't have it anymore. They did, like, tests on him and he doesn't have one piece of shit left in him. And why? Because he's not a fag or a freak." It must be nice to have enough money to be Magic. But I gotta tell you, in this life nobody has ever called me Magic. "Maybe, and don't get me wrong. But maybe, it's better this way. Get these fags and freaks off the street…" I gotta say somethin' straight here. It's not like this fuckin' sweater with a mouth isn't sayin' somethin' I wouldn't a said maybe a year ago. But it's just my girl, her head drops on my shoulder like it disconnected from her body. Like it ain't part of her anymore. And I looked at where she was lookin'. Right under this ad for 1-800-SKYDIVE is a shot of a G Q 'mo in a black tux and some chick who needs a cheeseburger in a long white dress. They're sellin' tampons or the lottery or somethin'. …And I know she's on that thing again. I mean, she ain't never had a new dress. Because something out of a box don't go to the Salvation Army… And when the hell is this army gonna start fightin' the Salvation war?

"Fags and freaks, who needs 'em?" But what freaks me out, like what ain't never happened to me before. With her head on my shoulder, I can't make a fist. My hand is as dead as a fish, or my guidance counselor's handshake.
"Fuck them."
Right at me.

OLD WOMAN: ...I remember in the morning, where you kept me, outside Rome... Outside? ...Living outside... never mind. I would open the window to smell the trees. Take the morning in. You know that's how you stay healthy. Take the day in, first thing. And it protects you till you sleep. ...It was, I loved the fig tree, its branch would just touch our balcony like a finger. I like it so much more than your ceiling. And through the leaves, through the shade, through the sun I would watch you get on your bicycle to go study. And you would turn to me and wink... And I would think to myself, "Look at my man in a dress. What a fool. Why is he going to study all day today when everything he ever needs to know in the world is in his wink?"

OLD MAN: Were you waiting for me?

OLD WOMAN: I was trying to cook! I don't know, I was chopping something, like an onion, when one of those turtle doves that kept us up at night flew in the house and I...

OLD MAN: Were you scared I wasn't coming back?

OLD WOMAN: I was waiting. I waited for you. And for weeks I kept waitin' for the right time to tell you. And when I did...I could see the lines in your eyes. Bloodshot. Like cracks. And you took off...I thought the door would come down off the hinges. And instead of soldiers it would be priests and bishops in robes and dresses, waving the papers. Screaming in Latin. Tellin' me they had you. And I was under arrest for being pregnant... Crimes against the church or something. But so, when the police came, hats off, and told me that your hands crashed into a wall, I didn't act surprised. I was relieved.

OLD MAN: I was always peddling so fast. Always sweating and runnin' and racin'...

OLD WOMAN: And you're still racing. You want to be the patron saint of bicycle races.

(The WOMAN *is dressed.)*

MAN: *(O S)* I made some...

WOMAN: *(To herself)* ...Where did...? How the...?

MAN: *(O S)* I found a hot plate and a...

WOMAN: Oh, no.

MAN: *(O S)* I don't know how people can live in a place without a kitchen. You want some?

WOMAN: Don't make a symphony out of it. You get those pots and pans going... —What the hell are you looking for?

MAN: *(O S)* I'm cooking.

WOMAN: I told you. I don't do that anymore. I told....

MAN: *(O S)* I'm cooking food!

WOMAN: Yeah?

MAN: *(O S)* ...You should eat....

WOMAN: ...You'll be here all night.

MAN: *(O S)* Two eggs are a very small tune.

WOMAN: I want you out by tonight.

MAN: *(O S)* What, you don't have time for an egg?

WOMAN: I oughta put a timer on you. Because no matter where you are, this is how it starts. That's it's, "Oh, do you got an onion...?" then oil you need, some spices, and it turns into a discussion about the history of the world.

(MAN *enters down left with a plate of scrambled eggs.*)

MAN: There's a black market in a downstairs on a backstreet, off of Mott Street in New York....

WOMAN: ...No...

MAN: ...It's behind this catering hall, for weddings and things....

WOMAN: ...No, no, no...

MAN: Where you can get any spice, oil or everything to make anything you could find in the world.

WOMAN: NO.

(MAN *bites into the eggs.*)

MAN: Shit!

WOMAN: What?

MAN: I just broke my tooth.

WOMAN: On an egg?

MAN: I been grinding my teeth, but...

WOMAN: Your mouth is bleeding.

MAN: I bit my tongue.

WOMAN: This is how it ends. It chips away. First it's your tooth. Then it's a bone. Then it's your personality. Then...

MAN: I must have left some shell in there....

WOMAN: Oh my God, do you hear that? You have a whistle in your speech. ...Do you hear me? We blink once or twice and we've lived our lives in a doorway. Married?! I can't even check out! You and me, we don't have a chance. Not a chance.

MAN: *(Tries to whistle)* I like it; it sounds like a little bird....

WOMAN: Why don't you understand "not a chance"?

MAN: Because I'm black.... *(Exiting down left)* You want some home fries?

BOY: *(On a recorded phone message)* "I'm me, so if you're you looking for me, then this is the right number. But if you ain't you, or I ain't me, hang the phone up...."

OLD WOMAN: Go to the basement and fix your damn chair already.

OLD MAN: What?

OLD WOMAN: Fix your chair!

OLD MAN: What chair? I don't know where it even is.

OLD WOMAN: It's in the basement! I just told you! Fix your fucking chair.

OLD MAN: I'm sitting here.

OLD WOMAN: You're sitting on your ass. Is that what happens when you get older, your brain drops into your ass?!

OLD MAN: I don't want to fix a chair.

OLD WOMAN: You got your own chairs to fix! In the basement. Broken. You still have things to fix. Even if you just go break it again! It's not right. People like us, with the same problems as us, fix their goddamn chairs. How dare you not fix 'em! What if I need a chair? What if we don't have enough chairs for dinner?!

OLD MAN: I'll stand!

BOY: Last message I got from my mother was like every message, for money. This is a photo of my Poppy at Kennedy. He had, like, a business trip. Look at him, wearin' a kiddy pilot hat and plastic wings on his shirt.

What a pussy. Last thing he did before he split was make a cheese sandwich with that government shit my mom hadda show her ass down at welfare to get. By then, we were sellin' food stamps at fifty to a dollar just to make a six-pack to watch Channel Nine. The only channel we had left.
The lights went out real quick in our house. One morning I'm waking up in a three-bedroom house up in Woodlawn, then we're in three rooms in the Bronx. Loud rooms. And he started throwin' shit out the window. Like the parakeet I won at this feast, this feast of lost causes. Oh, that bird was still in its cage when he threw it. But that's another thing....
He wrapped the sandwich in a plastic "I Love New York" bag, put a rubber band around it, and put it under his arm with the *Daily News*. He told my mother he was, like, going out for a pack of cigarettes or some stupid shit like that. I tell you, the minute a guy like this says he's goin' out for cigarettes, he ain't never comin' back. Outside, on the corner, he gave me a wink. I thought he was gonna give me some bullshit movie line like, "You're the man. Meet me in Saint Louis. Tora. Tora. Tora..." But no, he reached in his shirt pocket and tossed me a quarter. "That's my luck quarter." Which is bullshit. The fact is, he was checking phones all morning for loose change. Yeah, he's that guy. "Drop me a call." I wanted to drop it in the sewer. My mom lost her sense of humor when she lost my dad. Became a night lady to make ends meet. But those fuckin' ends don't ever meet. Slept all day. She always smelled like Mr Clean and old water.
Her hair got as dry as summer grass. I tellya, you put a match to that thing it woulda went up like a Jeannie. The only thing she talked about was the house in Woodlawn. I would climb up on this apple tree we had in the back, sit on a branch. She would sit in the shade

and whistle. Sometimes I'd throw a little apple at her and she would laugh. I left her the night she picked up an apple in her hand and cried her eyes out. I couldn't handle how much an apple hurt. But she stayed with me once, once a week, years ago. She stole all my money outta this old work book I kept it in. Learned my lesson. You gonna put money in a boot, make sure you got two boots 'cause one boot is like givin' it away. Me and my girl, we saw her recently over in Hell's Kitchen. We both made like we didn't know each other. Now that's got to hurt more than apples. And all that's left from my Poppy is a couple of postcards and a phone call or two he never finished 'cause he never had enough change for the pay phone. All I got is her....

(GIRL *goes through the flight instruction as if it were a dance.*)

GIRL: "In case of emergency, place the life jacket over your head and secure the tape firmly around your waist. Blow into the tube to inflate. Oxygen mask will drop down automatically."

BOY: *(Looking at the photo)* My Poppy got this insurance. Like you get a million dollars if his plane went down. But he never got it. Never took that business trip. Scared to fly. Man, he didn't even give us a chance.

GIRL: Pull the mask downward to begin the flow of oxygen. And adjust the strap firmly around your head. In case of an emergency landing, passengers should walk quickly to the emergency exits located at the back, center and front of the airplane. They found the black box. And they listen to it. And the pilot, his last words was, "Oh shit." ...Then he said....

(MAN *is ready to leave;* WOMAN *stands with him.*)

MAN: I love you.

WOMAN: Yeah…

MAN: Goodbye.

WOMAN: Goodbye.

MAN: Let's try it again. …Goodbye.

WOMAN: Goodbye.

MAN: Again. Goodbye.

WOMAN: Goodbye.

MAN: I'm not leavin' till you say it….

WOMAN: Say it how.

MAN: Say it like you don't want me to leave.

WOMAN: Goodbye.

MAN: …Goodbye.

WOMAN: Maybe you should just leave.

MAN: I'm not. Not until you say it right.

WOMAN: I'm sayin' it right because that's how I say it. Goodbye.

MAN: I'm not leaving.

WOMAN: Get out. GET OUT!

MAN: I'm lying down on this floor. I'm gonna sleep on my back. I'm gonna sleep on this floor, which is the most unnatural thing to do since we're supposed to sleep on beds. Until you say goodbye to me in the nice way. Goodbye.

WOMAN: Goodbye.

MAN: Not good enough. *(He lies down on the floor at the stage right end of the bed.)*

WOMAN: How about 'goodnight'?

MAN: That was nice. Why don't you say goodbye like that goodnight?

WOMAN: What don't you like, the good or the bye?

MAN: If you said that goodbye like that goodnight, well then I would leave.

WOMAN: Take the goodnight and leave.

MAN: No, goodnight is different than goodbye!

(WOMAN *sits on the bed and starts to cry.*)

MAN: What are you cryin' about?

WOMAN: Because you're an idiot.

MAN: Well, if I'm an idiot, I should be crying.

WOMAN: Idiot.

MAN: What?

WOMAN: You don't even know.

MAN: Know what?

WOMAN: It's not how I said "goodbye", it's how you said "I love you".

MAN: I love you.

WOMAN: No, it's no good now.

MAN: I love you is I love you.

WOMAN: But now I made you say it like that.

MAN: That's the way I meant it.

WOMAN: Say it again.

MAN: I love you. I love you. I love you.

(*Pause*)

WOMAN: Goodbye.

(GIRL *walks out in a beautiful white evening dress, sits in the stage center chair, and snaps out a cloth napkin and puts it on her lap.*)

GIRL: Where'd you get the dress?

BOY: Same place I got my tux.

MAN: Yeah, goodbye.

(*They kiss. He picks her up into his arms.*)

WOMAN: Goodbye.

GIRL: You forget people do things like get married.

BOY: Happy birthday.

(*The GIRL pulls out her gift-wrapped bag and puts it in front of her. Reveals a passport.*)

BOY: Happy birthday.

GIRL: I always wanted a passport.

BOY: I bought it from that junkie who nods out on the pier. The one, his nose almost touches the asphalt. He's made of twigs. Boy forgot how to eat. I bought his whole wallet, checkbooks and shit... He was a photographer. He was almost famous for, like, a year.

(GIRL *looks through the passport.*)

BOY: This place is so good, even Chinese people come here. How do you like the soup?

GIRL: What happens to that chicken when it loses at tic-tac-toe?

BOY: He goes in the soup.

GIRL: It tastes like medicine... It's nice to talk.

BOY: Every stamp is a place.

GIRL: What's Mad-a-ga-scar like?

BOY: They got leaves there as big as you.

GIRL: (*Looking through the passport*) Let's call her France.

BOY: You don't know it's a girl.

GIRL: She's not kickin', she's dancin'.

BOY: Jill. That's American.

GIRL: I hate Jack and Jill and Spot.

BOY: Names depress me.

GIRL: Let's call her Sassafrass…or Shiny Sumac….

BOY: Make it a somethin' small.

GIRL: She might live long, you don't know.

BOY: Otherwise the tombstone gets too expensive…

GIRL: You break my heart. *(She lets the napkin fall off her lap.)*

BOY: And when she went down for that napkin, I was gone.
Man, I don't wanna break her.
And what good am I to her if when she's around I can't even make a fist?

(BOY *to the audience as* GIRL *opens up a letter:*)

BOY: WHAT THE FUCK IS EVERYBODY LOOKIN' AT? DO YOU PEOPLE GOT ANY IDEA WHAT IT'S LIKE TO BE HUNGRY? NOT, LIKE, "Oh, I was so busy I forgot to eat today. I'm starvin'." I MEAN STARVIN' LIKE EATIN' A JAR OF WEEK-OLD PICKLES AND ROCK-HARD DONUTS OUT OF A DUMPSTER HUNGRY. SO HUNGRY YOU DON'T KNOW HOW TO WEAR A PARTY DRESS.
I went there that day to kill that doctor. He killed my girl. He's on my list… They all killed her, the test givers, the government fat-heads, the pharmacy pricks in their slick suits. And you fucks, every fuckin' one of you. You're all on my list!
When I was in school, they used to shovel this pile of coal in a hole in the floor outside, in the winter. I didn't think these rocks did shit. 'Cause it would be cold as hell in there. And this one time I said to the teacher, I said, "Fuck, it's cold as hell, lady."
And she said, "Sit on your hands. It'll keep you warm." That's why you're all on my list. It's fuckin' cold out here and you're all sittin' on your hands.

And then I saw her...

GIRL: Dear, no, to my girl...

BOY & GIRL: *(Together)* ...I will always remember your hair, 'cause with my face on it, like it was my pillow, I finally learned to sleep....

(GIRL *throws the letter down, pulls out a pair of scissors and starts cutting her hair.*)

BOY: First and maybe last letter I ever wrote.

(MAN *overlaps* BOY's *lines reciting recipe.*)

BOY: I shoulda sent her a cherry pie. That woulda said it better. That night, I hoped she was watchin' the eleven o'clock news. She would see the flames on the T V. The story about a house in Woodlawn that burned down. That old apple tree in the back caught first. The branch was so dead and dry. It lit up like a piece of paper. Lucky, the people that bought that house from my folks, they were on vacation. That house lit up like a Christmas tree on fire. A promise is a promise.

(MAN *finishes the last line of the recipe*)

BOY: And I promise you, the doctor is next....

MAN: Four ounces of raw peanuts.
Two dried jujube dates.
Five sliced fresh ginger.
One sliced karobi.
Three teaspoons of sesame oil.
One tablespoon of soy sauce.
Eight cups of water.
Two teaspoons of salt.
A pinch of sugar.
And one bird's nest from the other side of the wall...

(WOMAN *and* OLD MAN *sit at the table.* OLD WOMAN *is offstage.*)

OLD WOMAN: *(Offstage right)* Arrogance! He's gonna kill himself with arrogance.

OLD MAN: You need the code for the machines?

WOMAN: No, not now…

OLD MAN: You have the card in case you need money again.

OLD WOMAN: *(Offstage right)* He thinks he's so smart!

WOMAN: Mom!

OLD MAN: She's upset.

WOMAN: Why is she wearin' dark glasses?

OLD MAN: She won't tell you?

WOMAN: Very Jackie O!

OLD MAN: …Very dramatic. …She won't tell me.

OLD WOMAN: *(Offstage right)* ARROGANT!

OLD MAN: I love her temper. Did you know that?

WOMAN: No.

OLD MAN: I was always attracted to that temper. Whenever we had a problem, airline tickets or a bad check, a bill, she would just curse. Even back in Europe. Before it was fashionable…

OLD WOMAN: *(Offstage right)* Goddamn you!

WOMAN: Mom, is that helping?

OLD WOMAN: *(Offstage right)* That temper oughta smack you off the back of your arrogant head.

WOMAN: Mom…I didn't pack my striped shirt and whistle.

OLD WOMAN: *(Offstage right)* I can see you when I'm not even there.

WOMAN: Mom, I'm talkin' to him now!

OLD MAN: "Sunday…" that's the code.

WOMAN: Oh, thank you. ...How are you?

OLD MAN: How are you?

WOMAN: Fine.

OLD MAN: ...Fine.

WOMAN: Dad, I do not want to have a "fine" conversation.

OLD MAN: Where's the young man?

WOMAN: I wanted to talk to you first.

OLD MAN: I'm really fine....

WOMAN: He's a friend.

OLD MAN: Friend, or friend-friend?

WOMAN: We're friendly.

OLD WOMAN: *(Offstage right)* Tell her! Tell her about your friend... Your girlfriend. She's smart enough for you. She's your daughter and she's as arrogant as you....

WOMAN: Mom, for the last time... Please, for once! Lemme...please, on my own.

OLD WOMAN: *(Offstage right, to her daughter)* You know you are secretly arrogant.

WOMAN: Where are you?!

MAN: *(Offstage left)* I'm in the kitchen.

WOMAN: Mom, get in the kitchen. We have a guest.

OLD MAN: Get out of the bathroom! She's trying to cover up her eye... *(Whispers)* She's got a black eye. I don't know how.

OLD WOMAN: *(Offstage right)* All these years, he doesn't know who the real idiot is around here.

OLD MAN: Woman, don't make me angry.

OLD WOMAN: *(Offstage right)* You haven't been angry in a long time.

OLD MAN: Because I love you!

OLD WOMAN: *(Offstage right)* Bastard, I love you too, you sonovabitch....

OLD MAN: *(whispers)* It's so funny when she cusses. I tell you, it makes me laugh. Did you know that?

WOMAN: No.

OLD WOMAN: *(Offstage right)* If I was in shape... I'd slap you.

MAN: *(Offstage left)* I NEED A SAUCEPAN!

OLD WOMAN: Is he cookin'? Who is this man cookin' in my kitchen?

WOMAN: Mom, please...

MAN: *(Pans fall offstage left)* Shit...

WOMAN: *(To MAN)* Can you wait till I introduce you to them before you start cookin' in their kitchen?

OLD WOMAN: Who's cookin'?

WOMAN: Sometimes, I tell you, it's the only form of communication he has.

(Another pan falls.)

OLD WOMAN: Goddammit... He's going to dent things.

WOMAN: He's still a guest.

OLD WOMAN: Tell her about the girl. ...Excuse me! *(She exits down left.)*

OLD MAN: Bring me some water, please.

WOMAN: I'm sorry we're late... But, he literally carried me on the plane.

OLD MAN: Like newlyweds.

WOMAN: No. He stopped in Chinatown for some things.

OLD MAN: He's the man that answers the phone sometimes. God, we have so many numbers for you.

WOMAN: His shows up a lot.

OLD MAN: I was always scared we'd run out of numbers for you. ...Your life... Do you love him?

WOMAN: Who, him? ...Yeah, I guess. I—but he gets under my skin.

OLD MAN: That's where they go. As long as you love him, then I know you'll be okay. I know you don't think so, but you're good at love. He loves you.

WOMAN: You haven't even met him yet....

OLD MAN: ...he asked you for a pan.

(OLD WOMAN *reenters down left.*)

OLD WOMAN: Honey, he's black.

WOMAN: So?!

OLD WOMAN: So, nothing. It's just an observation. He's black... That's all.

(WOMAN *stares at her.* OLD WOMAN *exits down left.*)

OLD MAN: She's upset . . . all day.

WOMAN: You're not goin' to get rid of me. You're not just gonna make it alright. Because I got a man. Before you go and...

OLD MAN: What's all this about dying?

WOMAN: You're not eating.

OLD MAN: *(In a whisper)* I'm hallucinating... I been flying. Wild. I saw my parents this afternoon on a bicycle. They used to sit on it backwards, but pedal forward. I would laugh. He always bet on horses....

WOMAN: ...'Cause I'll split up with him right now. I'll walk away right now.

OLD MAN: Don't threaten me, honey.

WOMAN: I'm not. I just don't want you to make it easy for yourself.

OLD MAN: Don't threaten anyone with your own unhappiness.

WOMAN: *(Tears)* If you don't eat, you'll die.

OLD MAN: I know, but...I can't. I get so self-conscious. I...

WOMAN: Did something happen?

OLD MAN: Don't judge me for this, don't... For not eating and...

WOMAN: Dad, please, I just, I want to know... I need you and....

OLD MAN: And?

WOMAN: I don't feel...yet. Like... You were in your office and me and Mom waiting for you in the waiting room.

OLD MAN: All that waiting.

WOMAN: Sometimes Mom would say you were back from work even when you weren't.

OLD MAN: In the old days, that's what people did. Work.

WOMAN: I was always putting my ear up to people's chests to try and hear what you were doing in there.

OLD MAN: *(To himself)* Confession... *(To her)* How's that story you're working on?

WOMAN: Good. I mean, thanks for the image....

OLD MAN: ...I saw him out my window....

WOMAN: ...I got the boy up there. But, God, I don't know what to do with him. Maybe Mom is right; maybe it's just a hobby.

OLD MAN: Your mother talks in stories....

WOMAN: Do you like mine?

OLD MAN: They don't have to end so badly to get read.

WOMAN: Is the girl me?

OLD MAN: No. The boy in the sky. Falling. He's the girl's boyfriend.

WOMAN: What about the girl?!

OLD MAN: Somethin' came over me. I lost my reserve....

WOMAN: Is that good or bad?

OLD MAN: Call your mother.

WOMAN: DAD!

OLD MAN: Shh...

WOMAN: No.

OLD MAN: My whole life I kept the noises out of my room. People. I thought I knew how they sounded. Then, all of a sudden, I could listen to everything. I heard whispers like screams. Something like opening the window at my office. And then, the city with all that noise. I started hearing one sound at a time and it was just...it was like I never heard anything before.

WOMAN: Go to the country house.

OLD MAN: I married your mother. She's noisy, like a city.

WOMAN: Shut the window.

OLD MAN: Well, yes, exactly. That's it... But now it's my own life, the noise of my life...I'm tired of. I missed you, in my office back then… I'm sorry to you and your mother.

WOMAN: Dad, you gave us everything you had….

OLD MAN: And I gave you a sweet politeness. And you've been fighting it ever since. You know what a great doctor is? It's someone who impersonates a doctor exactly. Because if you care too much, if you're too aware, it feels all, it's just too much….

WOMAN: But, no…

OLD MAN: You know what is not a great man? A man who impersonates a man exactly… But that girl, so sweet, so pure.

WOMAN: That girl…was that sexual?

OLD MAN: Oh, as in memory maybe. As in a moment I remembered from long ago. …But.

WOMAN: She's dying?

OLD MAN: Lately, it's the only ones I get. Young and poor and no insurance. They come in, for a little light, for the opening in the window, a little hope. But hope means you don't know how it turns. We used to cure things, we… Things like now, they kill hope….

WOMAN: No, they can't. …Dad, I'm gonna be fine.

OLD MAN: She fell in love with a boy who didn't care and then he did. Like boys will. They didn't think. But kids that age shouldn't have to think. God, all this thinking. We can't even let our children be thoughtless anymore… They got tricked by…young and in love. And she got two things, sick and pregnant. But it was her hair.
I couldn't hear a thing she said. The look of it, the smell. …Does this make you uncomfortable?

WOMAN: …You?

OLD MAN: *(He smiles.)* I'm sorry. I should let you be uncomfortable with me. To just be that. I'm sorry about so many things... She was just talking. While it seemed so loud and clear how awful it was. I just touched her hair, just put my fingers through it. Why? To feel the hope, maybe. ...To hang on that.

WOMAN: Dad, I'm right here.

OLD MAN: She left so upset she didn't come back. I want to help her, and... But I didn't let it in.

WOMAN: Oh, Dad, Mom and I have hair. *(She leans toward him.)* You can touch my hair.

OLD MAN: I know. This poor girl. She was screaming about men. That she was gonna cut all her hair off. Shave her head. She wanted to be ugly. Our children want to be ugly. Why does everyone want to sleep with her? Why do they take so much out of her when she does...? But that wasn't it. It wasn't that. I love your mother and...

WOMAN: These things happen...we can't know why we act...but we have to.

OLD MAN: I was selfish, old, and scared of it. I wanted to feel her future. I should have been better.

WOMAN: Actions speak for themselves sometimes.

OLD MAN: No, I know, it's, she, rightfully so, she left. The world is cold and getting colder. She needed help. She didn't know how much I did too.... She's.... Her baby's dying. And I was.... I let her get close to me. There is so much I haven't said, or worse, felt, for me...for you... I watched myself for so long; I don't like what I saw. You see, the thing is I was fine. I thought I was fine. It was weeks I was tying my tie and I pulled off one of her hairs. And the moment I touched it, the tears that came out of me. Years worth. I felt everything about her, it was like I knew every feeling and every thought she ever had. And she was so lacking in hope. I cried. Your mother was hysterical. She never saw me like that. But I felt this girl. You see, that hair was my hope, that she had hope, but… How can you help someone if you know they they have no hope? If you have none…?

WOMAN: And what if, what if, just what if you just don't…know there is no hope for her? You don't know everything. Mom is right; that is so arrogant.

OLD MAN: What if I do?

(OLD WOMAN *enters down left, dark glasses off.*)

OLD WOMAN: I knew it. I knew it. You bastard. If you married me to scream for you…? I won't anymore!

OLD MAN: This is not about you. This is about me!

OLD WOMAN: You are about me!

WOMAN: *(She looks at her mother's eye)* Mom! Sit down. How many rounds did it go?

OLD WOMAN: Oh, it was nothin'… I was going to the market. Because I'm the one who goes out around here. …It felt like an accident, really, but it wasn't… Across the street.

BOY: I gave her the look. And with my mind I says to her, "come and try to fuck with me." The "I'm gonna take you down" look.

OLD WOMAN: Lookin' like that. His eyes were wide like a baby who's seen somethin' they've never seen before. Somethin' I felt was down in me. Pulled me in and to him… *(To* WOMAN*)* He was coming for your father. I knew it. …I wanted to get as close as possible to him without touching him. I wanted to smell him, but…

BOY: I stepped off the curb. Between a truck and a car. I don't…in my head I was, "come right at me." Come on you old money-bag-hag-Macy's-perfume-smellin'…

OLD WOMAN: …I went right for him. Right at him. And I thought he was scared. This kid, this kid I walk by each day. Is he scared of me?

BOY: And I was scared. I rocked my body away.

OLD WOMAN: And I went at him.

BOY: But I rocked back. 'Cause I don't fuckin' like bein' scared of anyone or anything.

OLD WOMAN: I stood in his path.

BOY: In my way.

OLD WOMAN: We stared at each other. Like a stare before a kiss. A stare that says, "No matter how hard your heart hits, it's all okay."

BOY: Starin' at me so hard, my eyes got wet. I couldn't see anything good. It was all gettin' blurry, like lookin' in the rain. Everything shaky, everything still.

OLD WOMAN: A slow stillness. Like for once in my life, no one else existed. And in it I thought, "My God, oh my God. Look at the two of us, here, from two worlds getting further away." Not knowing a thing about each other except a desire to kiss. A fear, the last time I felt, before my child was born.

BOY: And I ripped the chain right off her neck!

OLD WOMAN: And I ripped his chain right off his neck!

BOY: Bitch took my Christ-head. Thing cost me over a hundred, and that's on the street. What a Christ-head costs at a place like Tiffany's or somethin', fuck knows.

OLD WOMAN: He took my Star of David. Remember, you got it for me from that old five and dime on Second Avenue? Every time I would lose that star, it would turn up somewhere. But, I mean, it's worthless except to me....

(The BOY *throws a punch, hitting the old woman on the upstage side of her face.)*

OLD WOMAN: I thought, what kinda world do we live in where a boy punches an old woman like me?

BOY: Yeah, what kinda world is it where a punk-ass bullshit artist like me has got to punch some old woman in the face? *(To the audience)* Just to tell you ass-holdin' fuckers how I feel!

OLD WOMAN: *(Showing her Christ-head)* How do you like my Christ-head?

BOY: *(Opens his fist to show his Star of David)* My star? And if I make it, I'm gonna give it to my girl.

GIRL: Hope is a tree.
Nests go in trees.
Birds grow in nests.
I call this bird "hope."
(She unwraps the box. From it, she pulls out a tiny cage that has a little bird in it. She collects her hair off the bed and floor, putting it into the box. She takes the get-well card, pulls out a pen, and reads what she is writing.)
Dear Doctor,
This is for you. Take it. I need your help more than I need my hair.

OLD WOMAN: THIS IS WHAT YOU WERE LOOKING FOR? FOR FORTY YEARS AND IT'S BEEN COMING INTO YOUR OFFICE EVERY DAY?!

OLD MAN: I can't believe I didn't tell her. They have cocktails now. Recipes that can save children.

WOMAN: Daddy, maybe she'll find you.

OLD MAN: She flew in and I closed the door and I tried to catch her.

OLD WOMAN: In Italy, when a bird flies into your house you're supposed to jam a knife in your dining room table, open all the windows and ask the bird to fly. The knife is for protection against evil spirits and such. Because if a bird dies in your house, it's bad luck.

WOMAN: Or maybe we should find her.

(The OLD MAN looks at his daughter and smiles. OLD MAN, OLD WOMAN and WOMAN sit in silence as MAN enters down left holding a bowl of steaming soup as he crosses to center stage.)

MAN: ...How's it goin'?

(The WOMAN looks as if she could kill him.)

MAN: ...Can cut it with a knife. ...I'll wait in the, in the...

OLD MAN: What do you do?

MAN: Me? I, it's kinda crazy, but it makes sense. I have degrees in anthropology. I'm from Los Angeles, but what I do is I travel around the world looking for indigenous recipes. A lot of people don't take it so seriously.

OLD WOMAN: *(To WOMAN)* He made a mess....

MAN: *(Looking around)* My mother cooked and cleaned in a house like this.

WOMAN: Not now... *(To MAN, in a whisper)* Sometimes you make me so angry....

MAN: You people don't know angry till you spend a day in my skin.

OLD MAN: No, please, what do you do?

MAN: I collect the recipes. I mean, like, I just came back from a trip to China. A province near the wall. This stuff is like, inedible... No, you gotta have a taste for it. Like, there's this bird's nest soup from this area and,

I knew in New York I would find the ingredients. It's not exactly the same, but it's close, maybe better. You still get that other world thing....

WOMAN: Is he upsetting you?

OLD MAN: No...

MAN: Sorry, it's just that food to me is, like, the ultimate act of civilization. I have a theory that the Italian Renaissance was really started with a tomato. Food is communication on, like, this immediate level. I understand fasting, from Yom Kippur to Matthew 17:20, is considered the highest form of praying....

WOMAN: *(To herself)* ...Oh, God...

MAN: ...But, if you love someone, you can even remember their taste, really. I'm goin' on... I'll just wait....

OLD MAN: What do you have there?

MAN: Bird's nest soup...

(MAN *reaches the bowl out to the* OLD MAN, *who takes it, smells it, and looks in the bowl.*)

OLD WOMAN: Smells good...?

WOMAN: *(To the* OLD WOMAN*)* Shhh!

MAN: Yeah, here it's a delicacy, but over there... One man's delicacy is another man's meal... The pot they use in the region is bent, dented. A hundred years old. There is no way to replace that.

OLD WOMAN: Maybe a little paprika.

WOMAN: Mom...

MAN: No. Yes, maybe a little paprika would taste like a pot like that.

OLD WOMAN: What's so funny, little miss burn-my-hand-in-the-kitchen?

WOMAN: I just love that word 'paprika.'

MAN: Me too. *(He exits down left into the kitchen.)*

GIRL: *(Writing)* ...This hair is payment towards my next visit. I forgive if you can.

(MAN reenters down left with paprika.)

MAN: Paprika!

(MAN puts some paprika in the bowl. The OLD WOMAN feeds the OLD MAN. He starts to eat the soup.)

BOY: ...I just thought of somethin'. This is the first time I ever been in the country. Even if it's coming at me at like thousands of miles per second. The fresh air was never this fast....

GIRL: *(To the audience. Touching her belly)* We could call her Hope. They say, love is the opposite of hate. I say, hope is the opposite. Hope. Hope is...

BOY: Everybody knows, right? That people don't fly they fall? Do you fuckers think I died? You think I hit that floor like roadkill. But maybe I didn't. And I'll give you three reasons why. One, just 'cause no one's survived from a height like this don't mean I won't. A wind could just come and pick me right up. Two, fuckers like me don't die. And three, she loves me, she loves me so good she might just keep me alive. To be continued and fuck you.

(The GIRL opens the cage and lets the bird fly into the audience. The OLD WOMAN picks up the ice pick, left earlier on the table and stabs it into the top of the table.)

OLD MAN: Open the windows.

(The MAN crosses downstage and opens the windows as the OLD MAN reaches across the table and puts his hand on his daughter's head.)

GIRL: Hope is.... Hope is....

WOMAN: It's alright. I can hear your heart....

(The WOMAN *reaches out and takes the* OLD WOMAN'S *hand. The* OLD WOMAN *takes the* OLD MAN'S *hand. The* MAN *picks up the white cloth napkin the* GIRL *dropped earlier onto the floor up center.)*

MAN: You left this on the plane. You were writing on it. She's really good.... *(He snaps open the white cloth napkin. He reads off of it.)* And it was alright. When the wind picked up the falling boy. Held him in its arms like he never had been as a child, for a moment, to say alright. And then, as he fell through the tree each branch tried to grab him. Hopefully. And breaking his fall. But it wasn't until he was under the lake's water that he finally felt like he was flying. Floating up to where the blue of the water met the blue of the sky. And when he broke through for air, it was her name he screamed. It was her he wanted to breathe in. She knows how to live.

GIRL: *(She pulls out a necklace she is wearing. The Star of David)* "Hope is the thing with feathers..." —Emily Dickinson.

END OF PLAY

www.ingramcontent.com/pod-product-compliance
Lightning Source LLC
Chambersburg PA
CBHW071750040426
42446CB00012B/2511